THE COLOURED HORSE AND PONY

CONTENTS

GW00685376

INTRODUCTION

Coloured horses and ponies have grown enormously in popularity over recent years and can now be found performing in all spheres of equestrian activities and sports. Increasingly, coloured horses and ponies are benefiting from well-considered breeding programmes that are retaining and improving on quality, type and conformation as primary considerations. From the traditional, coloured vanner to the coloured international sport horse, each has its place in twenty-first century equestrianism and deserves to be of the best possible quality for its given purpose.

It is hugely rewarding for those of us who have been in the vanguard of promoting the coloured horse and pony over the years to see these developments embraced by the equestrian community as a whole and I am confident that the future augurs well for the welfare, breeding, success and longevity of coloured horses and ponies throughout the UK. It is with great enthusiasm therefore that I write the introduction to this guide to coloured horses and ponies.

The term 'coloured', of course, is a catch-all that encompasses a vast array of particular colours, markings and types, and this guide reflects the extent of this range. While this book does not claim to be the most exhaustive on the subject, it gives a general overview of colours and types, as well as a useful introduction to showing. It will serve as a valuable source of information for those who are new to coloured horses and ponies as well as providing a factual reference point for the more experienced horse owner.

Finally, I would encourage anyone who is interested in the welfare, breeding and performance of coloured horses and ponies to join one of the equestrian societies devoted to this purpose. For it is only through combining our efforts, expertise and horsemanship that we can continue to develop the quality and status of coloured horses and ponies in this country.

Caroline Hamilton
Chair, CHAPS (UK)

COLOUR AND MARKINGS

Coloured horses or ponies are quite simply those that have white patches on their bodies, above the level of the stifle or elbow, together with at least one other colour. They can vary from being almost totally white with just a small amount of another colour in patches – extended pied – to almost totally dark with just a small patch or two of white – minimal pied. Sometimes they may also be referred to as broken coloured or parti-coloured.

PIEBALD AND SKEWBALD

The main colour names in use in Britain until recent years were piebald and skew-bald. Piebald can only be used to denote black and white.

Skewbald, however, can be used for absolutely any other colour and white. Most commonly, the term 'skewbald' has been used to mean brown or bay and white.

The terms piebald and skewbald tell us nothing, however, about the animal's markings. More recently the terms **tobiano** and **overo** have come into use and these tell us about the nature and origin of the horse or pony's markings. By using these terms along with colour names we can describe the coloured horse or pony more accurately.

TOBIANO

Tobiano applies when the white is dorsal in origin, i.e. the white starts at the top of the horse's back or neck. The legs are usually white up to above the knees and hocks as in the adjacent picture.

The darker coloured patches usually include some or all of the head, chest and flanks. The best way to think of the typical tobiano pattern is to imagine that a pot of white paint has been poured over the horse or pony from above, although there are of course many variations.

Another way to think of the tobiano is as having a white base that includes the back, with large patches of colour.

A look around any horse show will tell you that tobiano is the most common of the colour patterns in the UK. Using combinations of colour and marking descriptions, we can now begin to describe more accurately the coloured horse or pony as in the examples below.

Tovero is the term used to describe a mixture of tobiano and overo.

The more unusual colours have more unusual descriptions.

The pony here (right) is lemon and white, or lemon tobiano; palomino tobiano is another term used for this colouring.

When the lemon or palomino tobiano colouring is teamed with a black mane and tail, the colour is known as a dun or buckskin tobiano.

Grey and white colouring as in the picture below is often referred to as blue tobiano or blue and white because, as the name suggests, the effect is a blue tinge.

OVERO

Overo markings are less common in the UK than tobiano, but are particularly prevalent in both North and South America. Overo describes markings that are ventral in origin, i.e. the exact opposite of tobiano in that they originate underneath the horse's or pony's belly, or low down on the animal's side, with the darker colour extending the full length of the spine from the ears to the top of the tail.

The most common overo colour is chestnut, although any colour combination is possible.

There are three main patterns of overo that further define the nature of the markings.

Frame Overo

The frame overo is perhaps the least common pattern seen in horses and ponies in the UK, although it is found frequently in North and South America. As the name suggests, the animal's white markings are literally framed by a darker-coloured outline.

The overo's legs are usually dark and the dark colour typically extends up the horse's chest and underneath the neck at the front, and up through the tail and along the full length of the spine from the back. The face may or may not have white markings.

AUTHOR'S TIP

H.M. the Queen has made a significant contribution to the public profile of coloured horses in this country with her coloured stallions Oberon and Mars(below), now owned by Mrs M. Timmis.

AUTHOR'S TIP

Sometimes it is impossible to decide exactly which pattern of overo best describes a horse or pony's markings as the overo pattern can be very mixed and extremely variable, in which case it is best just to describe the animal as overo.

Splashed Overo

The splashed overo usually has a white belly, chest and flanks, with mostly white legs, and white extending round the head, including the eye area.

The eyes are typically blue and the tail is often dark at the top and white lower down. Although the term is 'splashed', it looks more like the horse or pony has been dipped, nose down, into white paint. The upper part of the body and the full length of the spine from the ears to the top of the tail are of the darker colour.

Sabino Overo

Like the splashed overo, the sabino has a white belly that may extend up both sides of the body and, perhaps confusingly, really does look as though it has splashed about in a puddle of paint. The distinguishing feature is that the edges of the white markings are mottled or spotted, sometimes also fading into roan patches.

The legs usually show high-level white, up above the hocks and knees, and the underside of the neck is splashed with white that may extend down the chest and through the forelegs and up under the jaw. The face and head may be partly or entirely white, and the eyes may be either blue or dark.

The sabino is the most common and most variable overo pattern in horses and ponies in the UK, occurring frequently in Welsh ponies (predominantly Sections A and D of the stud book), and may arise even from single colour parents with no apparent overo bloodlines. The pony below is a sabino with Welsh Section D breeding.

BREED AND TYPE

There is no actual breed of horse or pony indigenous to the UK that is specifically or exclusively coloured. Indeed, only one of the twelve officially recognized UK native breeds includes coloured ponies in its registered stud book: the Shetland.

Historically speaking, the closest we might once have come to identifying a breed of coloured horse or pony in Britain is perhaps with the traditional vanner, or gypsy horse. Due to the nomadic existence and irregular breeding of this animal, however, no records exist that would ever enable a breed to be officially recognized.

Likewise in the USA and in other parts of the world, there is, arguably, no actual breed of coloured horse or pony, though the American paint and pinto have in recent years acquired breed status.

We must therefore dispel any notion of a unified, coloured breed and think rather of coloured horses and ponies in terms of **types**.

There are in fact as many types of parti-coloured horse

and pony as there are of solid-coloured types. Type is determined largely by the purpose for which the animal's size, conformation and characteristics make it most suitable. That being the case, it is impossible here to cover every activity for which a coloured horse or pony might be used, so we confine ourselves to the most prevalent types. Indeed such is the versatility of our horses and ponies that a great many are suitable for a number of different purposes, and the boundaries between one type and another are often somewhat blurred.

STALLION GRADING

The grading of stallions plays an important role in the preservation and continuous improvement of type, conformation and quality of coloured horses and ponies. If a horse or pony has graded status, a breeder can be assured that it meets exacting standards that have been set and assessed by a team of experts, including veterinarians.

To pass the grading, each equine must be examined for excellent conformation, outstanding performance ability and perfect health. CHAPS (UK) holds two grading events each year that put both mares and stallions through this rigorous assessment before admitting them to the register of graded animals. The very best of the best are awarded 'elite' status through their performance record in one of the Olympic disciplines or through sustained outstanding performance in the show ring.

Experts agree that it is highly desirable to breed using only graded stallions. As the range of stallions presented for grading expands to include more types, this approach becomes ever more practicable.

NATIVE

The only pure-bred British native pony that may be coloured is the Shetland and this is true for both the standard and miniature Shetlands. Thus the coloured Shetland pony has been an influence in the development of small native-type coloured ponies by crossbreeding with other small breeds.

The coloured native-type pony should bear the hardy characteristics common to the twelve recognized British native pony breeds: good bone, short-coupled, with a well-set head and neck, small ears and a keen eye; it should not look like a small horse, but very much a pony, with a free-flowing mane and tail and silky feather at the fetlocks, but without the abundance or length of mane, tail and feather of the vanner and traditional types.

Perhaps the most easily identified coloured natives are those of Welsh pony origin, produced from crossbreeding with any section of the Welsh stud book. In a few rare cases a Welsh Section A pony has been produced with sabino colouring that has been eligible for dual registration both as a pure-bred Welsh pony and as a coloured pony. This is very much the exception, however.

The native-type horse is altogether more difficult to define. For while there are many breeds of horse that originate in the British Isles, when we speak of British Native breeds we commonly mean the twelve pony breeds. The Welsh Section D, however, has no official upper height limit, although it is still technically a pony. Thus the native-type horse is often of Welsh Section D extraction and while standing at over 148 cm (14.2 hh) in height shares many characteristics with the smaller native-type pony.

VANNER AND TRADITIONAL

These are the strongly built, draught-type animals of the coloured horse and pony world: deep-girthed, broad-chested, strong-limbed and capable of carrying or pulling large loads.

The distinction between a vanner and a traditional type is something of a grey area. Generally speaking vanners are the larger heavyweights, over 148 cm (14.2 hh), that are used for draught purposes, but many of these can be equally well shown under saddle and referred to as traditionals. The traditional type is in essence similar to the vanner, but used for riding purposes rather than as a draught animal. Both have abundant, flowing manes and tails and full, thick feathers that reach up as far as the back of the knee.

Smaller traditionals are more easily defined in that by virtue of their size they cannot be confused with the much larger vanner.

AUTHOR'S TIP

The vanner was historically the horse of choice for Romany travellers since its distinctive markings made ownership easy to identify and it was capable of carrying an entire family on its broad back as well as pulling a caravan. Indeed, while a short back was generally thought desirable in draught horses, the opposite was true of a vanner, since its back might have to accommodate two adults and several children on short journeys to town when the caravan was encamped.

DRIVING COB

Coloured cobs are popular for pleasure driving and are often used for ride and drive competitions. The action of the driving cob is frequently rounded and high, with particularly extravagant hock and knee action.

RIDDEN/SHOW COB

The coloured show cob stands at around the 153–155 cm (15–15.1 hh) mark, though smaller animals are also acceptable. This coloured type is in the currently unique position of being equally well represented in show cob classes that are not exclusive to coloured exhibits as his solid-coloured counterparts. All that is true of the solid-coloured cob applies equally to the coloured cob.

The ridden or show cob is a weight-carrying animal with a deep girth, short back, generous quarters and short cannon bones. Its action should be lower than that of the driving cob and, more than any other type of equine, the show cob must be the very paragon of impeccable manners.

The show cob is always presented hogged and trimmed and with feathers clipped out as in the picture below.

AUTHOR'S TIP

Well into the middle of the twentieth century, a coloured driving cob would always sell well to tradesmen for the job of pulling a cart. It is easy to imagine that a striking, vividly coloured horse or pony would catch the public's attention when pulling a butcher's or baker's cart and would serve as an excellent advertisement for a trade.

HUNTER, SHOW HUNTER AND WORKING HUNTER

For most of the twentieth century a coloured horse or pony was a rare sight in the hunting field, where it was thought to be too noticeable, but by the late twentieth century, any hunt was likely to have its fair representation of coloured hunters. This is increasingly reflected in the show ring where, in working hunter classes, a coloured horse or pony will stand out remarkably from a line of mostly bay and chestnut exhibits but still be competing on equal terms.

The hunter types are riding animals that combine the speed and stamina to sustain a full day's hunting with plenty of bone and powerful hind-quarters to withstand the rigours of negotiating a range of obstacles.

All hunter types need to have a long, ground-covering stride and should be able to give a strong, forward-going gallop without being out of control.

For showing purposes these types are always turned out with manes plaited and tails either plaited or pulled.

RIDING PONY, SHOW PONY, HACK AND RIDING HORSE

These types are at the finer end of the weight scale and are used more or less exclusively for riding and showing purposes, where elegance and refinement are paramount. They should display a free-flowing, graceful and low action.

The riding types include the child's lead-rein pony standing at up to 122 cm (12 hh) and, at the opposite end of the height scale, the large riding horse at anything around 163 cm (16 hh).

The show pony, at any height up to 148 cm (14.2 hh), is somewhat finer of bone and lighter in overall build than the show hunter pony. Similarly, the hack is the lighter equivalent in the horse category.

The riding, show and hack types, like the hunter types, are always shown plaited and trimmed and with pulled or plaited tails.

All the requirements for solid-coloured animals of these types are the same for coloured animals. The coloured show pony and hack still have some way to go, however, in being accepted on equal terms in the show ring alongside solid-coloured animals in the way that cobs and working hunter types are.

SPORT HORSE/PONY, WARMBLOOD AND PERFORMANCE HORSE/PONY

These are the athletes of the equine world and there is nothing that can be said about the solid-coloured animals in these classifications that cannot also be said about the coloured representatives of those same classifications. They are the show jumpers, dressage horses and eventers that combine athleticism, agility, stamina, speed and power for top performance. These horses and ponies are highly trained, responsive, obedient, intelligent and courageous.

All performance and sport horses and ponies need to have powerful hindquarters, strong, sloping shoulders, good bone and plenty of heart and lung room.

Coloured warmblood horses from mainland Europe have been a particularly strong influence on breeding programmes in the UK where power and performance are paramount.

AMERICAN BREEDS

There are increasing numbers of American coloured horses and ponies in the UK and their breed status is often misunderstood.

The official pinto register in the USA accepts any American breed or type of horse or pony that is of broken colour. The pinto register is therefore essentially a record of colour and not of a single, unified breed. It does, however, classify pintos according to type within the register.

For the non-expert, 'pinto' conjures up an image of a mustang or Native American type pony of broken colour with very specific pony characteristics of light build, speed and agility.

The American paint has gained status as a breed in recent years, though this status is still debated by some. Academically speaking the American paint could be argued to be a type, since it is derived from Quarterhorse and Thoroughbred bloodlines, but then many so-called pure breeds have been subject to this type of influence over the centuries, either through natural evolution or the intervention of man. Unlike the Pinto Association, The American Paint Horse Association admits animals only of verified and acceptable bloodlines since its concern is with breeding rather than colour *per se*.

The American Saddlebred is one of the few breeds globally that admits coloured horses to its studbook as pure bred.

SHOWING YOUR COLOURED HORSE OR PONY

There is no reason why the coloured horse or pony cannot compete in all spheres alongside solid-coloured equines, according to type and suitability. If your local show does not include a separate class for coloured horses and ponies you should not let this deter you from entering whatever event you feel would suit you and your horse or pony.

As coloured horses and ponies increase in popularity, however, so too there are increasing opportunities to compete in show classes dedicated specifically to coloured exhibits. The number and type of classes devoted entirely to coloured horses and ponies depend on the size and nature of the show.

Local and clubs' shows generally have a minimum of one in-hand and one ridden class for coloured equines. Many of these shows now offer an opportunity to qualify for the CHAPS (UK) championship shows as well as other regional and national championships.

There are also whole shows devoted exclusively to coloured horses and ponies that are run by CHAPS (UK) all over the country. Some of these, together with other larger and county shows, offer the best horses and riders a chance to qualify for the CHAPS (UK) ridden finals at the prestigious Horse of the Year Show.

Other showing societies also run special classes and championship series for coloured horses and ponies. These include the British Skewbald and Piebald Association and Ponies Association (UK), which runs both summer and winter championship series in-hand and under saddle for coloured exhibits.

RIDDEN CLASSES

Ridden showing classes at larger shows are generally split into two or four sections, and this is certainly true of qualifying classes for the Horse of the Year Show. Thus there are separate classes for horses and ponies, and then each is divided into one class for native, traditional and cob types, and another for riding, hack/show pony and hunter types.

At some of the very large shows such as the CHAPS (UK) Championships there are separate ridden classes for each individual type as well as separate classes for Shetlands, veterans, novices, side-saddle and equitation.

This is very likely to expand as the popularity and number of coloured equines grows.

Increasingly, shows also include working hunter classes for coloured horses and ponies that culminate in a national final.

The colour and markings of the animal are not a consideration in any ridden classes with CHAPS (UK) (though this does vary with other showing societies): the judge is looking for quality, conformation, performance and manners.

AUTHOR'S TIP

Young and novice horses and ponies should be shown in a snaffle bridle as shown below left.

Generally plain browbands are worn by natives, cobs, traditional types and hunters, with fancy browbands being worn by show ponies, riding horses and hacks.

Experienced horses and ponies and those competing in open classes should be shown in a bridle with two reins – either a double bridle (below right) or Pelham bridle. It is always advisable to seek professional help when using one of these for the first time as a poor fit and misuse can lead to problems.

IN-HAND CLASSES

As with the ridden showing classes, at larger shows and CHAPS (UK) shows, in-hand classes are generally split into separate classes for horses and ponies and according to type.

A unique feature of in-hand classes is that both local shows and larger shows often have a separate class or number of classes for youngstock up to three years of age, as well as for foals and brood mares.

In these classes the judge is looking for quality, conformation and type. Manners are less of a consideration, but a horse or pony should always be well behaved and under control; if it is not the exhibitor may be asked to leave the ring.

Again, colour and markings are not specific considerations in most in-hand classes but, as they might be in some classes, it is a good idea to check the rules for each showing society. The main exception to this is the class that appears in the show schedule as 'Best Colour

and Markings'. It is generally only in these classes that colour and markings take precedence over quality, conformation and trueness to type.

SPORT AND PERFORMANCE CLASSES

It is rare for a show or competition to include separate sport and performance classes for coloured equines, but the CHAPS (UK) annual championship show is a major occasion on which these equine athletes compete without solid-coloured competitors.

Classes include in-hand performance and sport horse/pony types, with separate sections for youngstock, and classes with huge spectator appeal such as loose jumping, style and performance, combined training and dressage.

CHILDREN'S CLASSES

CHAPS (UK), along with other showing and breed societies, is keen to support and encourage young riders. A number of show classes cater exclusively for the very young. There are lead-rein classes for riders up to eight years of age, and first-ridden classes for riders up to twelve years of age that culminate in finals at the CHAPS (UK) Championships.

Additionally there are classes for young handlers and novelty classes such as Bonny Pony. These classes introduce children to in-hand showing from an early age and offer even those who have not yet mastered the rising trot an opportunity to experience the thrill of the show ring.

CONCLUSION

This short work has given an insight into the history and development of coloured horses and ponies in the UK, as well as explaining their current position in terms of colour, markings, type and showing. While it has not been possible here to cover every item in depth, or to discuss the more specialized aspects of breeding, it has been shown that coloured horses and ponies have their place not only in the equestrian heritage of the UK, but also very much in its future.

AUTHOR'S TIP

Pegasus, the winged horse of ancient mythology, has been represented in art throughout the ages as being of a silvery grey colour. The artist Rubens, in the early seventeenth century, however, depicted Pegasus as a bay tobiano, giving the coloured horse its place in legend.

COLOURED HORSE AND PONY SOCIETY (UK)

Further information about joining CHAPS (UK) and about the society's shows, stallion grading and other areas of activity can be found at:

www.chapsuk.com

Or by telephoning:
01685 845045

Or by writing to:
CHAPS (UK),
1 McLaren Cottages,
Abertysswg,
Rhymney,
Tredegar
NP22 5BH

ACKNOWLEDGEMENTS

The author is grateful to all those who have contributed to the production of this book both financially and by the provision of photographs and other help, in particular CHAPS (UK) for generously sponsoring the production costs.

Photographs were contributed by members of CHAPS (UK) and also selected from the Society's own archives. Where copyright does not belong to the CHAPS (UK) member the author has tried to identify all copyright holders and seek permissions. The author and CHAPS (UK) wish to thank the following individuals for providing photographs featured in this work and the named photographers for their permission to reproduce their photographs.

Julie Cameron, Amanda Chapman, Sherri and Emily Church, Lyndsey Cox, S. Davies, Gillian Deane, Rachel Dickinson, Bethany Driver, Sally Eyre, Donna Foxcroft, Sarah and James Frith, Maria McGahan, Eve Gorman, Caroline Hamilton, Taira Iqbal, Bradley Jones, C. Jones, Jennifer Keepe, Heather Linfield, Julie Mallett, Daikin Marsh, Barry Mawdsley, Claire Merrigan, Carla Michalik, Deborah Mitchell, Philippa Porley, Leane and Michelle Pickford, Joan Riding-Smith, Jane Rodgers, Sally-Ann and Charlotte Rose, Mark Shaw, Phil Smith, Brenda Thompson, Jayne Thompson, Mrs M. Timmis, Stephanie Towers, Sally Shaw, Felicity Spencer.

Real Time Imaging, Fotograffs, Penelope Barlow, Anthony Reynolds, Cherry-Ann Wilde, K. Ettridge, Neil B. Jones, Helen Revington, Richard Weller-Poley, Mark R. Heath, John Britter, Steve Webber, Jessie Ambridge, Mike Freeman, Mike Arnold.

The author acknowledges the work of Carole Knowles Pfeiffer on horse and pony coat colours and would refer readers to this work for further information: *Horse and Pony Coat Colours*, Carole Knowles Pfeiffer, published by J. A. Allen (London, 2000).

British Library Cataloguing-in-Publication Data.
A catalogue record for this book is available from the British Library

ISBN-10: 0-85131-917-3
ISBN-13: 978-0-85131-917-9

Published in Great Britain in 2005 by
J. A. Allen an imprint of Robert Hale Ltd.,
Clerkenwell House, 45–47 Clerkenwell Green,
London EC1R 0HT

Design and Typesetting by Paul Saunders
Series editor Jane Lake
Printed by Gutenberg Press Limited, Malta